EVERYDAY DEMONS

One Woman's Hell

A Memoir

By

MeLinda Smith

blakgirl publishing.com, Inc. ™
Book designed by blakgirl publishing.com, Inc.

To order additional copies of this book, contact:

blakgirl publishing.com, Inc.
1-516-255-5249
(fax) 1-516-255-5279
www.blakgirl publishing.com
Hilda@bgirlpub.com

This book is dedicated to my mother. May God continue to restore your life and give you peace in your heart and in your home.

Table Of Contents

CHAPTER ONE

The Roots Of Weeds

On May 12, 1991 I stopped drinking...no more alcohol for me. From then on, I would drink lots of water. That was the plan. I thought it was a good plan because all that liquor has probably pickled my organs. Then, on May 13th, I remembered that I drank in order to forget. That day, I had beer...lots of beer. In hindsight, I can say that drinking didn't solve anything. Whenever I felt that things were not going the way that I wanted them to, I tried to make them better. Unfortunately, every time I tried to better the situation it would only get worse. When things got worse, I would drink. Then, I would keep drinking. I would drink even when I tried my best to avoid doing so. I was hurting, and my pain was like a fire burning deep within me. I would spend all day drinking, and the purpose of each drink was to put out that fire. Problem is, each time I tried to douse the fire with alcohol, the flames would grow. I must have been out of my mind because to me larger flames meant I needed a larger amount of drink. I just kept feeding that fire in an effort to extinguish it.

I was alone in this world. I never thought that one could be surrounded by family and still be so alone. Not many folks have heard of High Springs, Florida, but my family has so many ties to this tiny town. My mother and grandmother lived here for decades before giving up the Ghost. One of my brothers lived here, but he died of suspicious circumstances. (He caught a bullet with his head, and his death was deemed a suicide.) My youngest sister lived here most of her life, but in June of last year she too passed. I still look after her four kids and her grandchild just as I did when she was ailing. I have five children of my own. All but one are now adults: my firstborn son is no longer with us... he was 22 years old when he was knifed to death. In any case, both litters are as selfish as they wanna be. How could so many children turn out to be so rotten? They're against me, and they're against each other. I really need to let go of this mob I raised for Satan because I'm tired. I'm tired of the headaches, and I'm tired of the heartache.

My mother's conniving sister has been here for centuries. With her hair pulled and pinned upward before cascading into a garden of salt-and-pepper curls above her brow, she has always *looked* like a dignified elder. Her casual clothing elegantly drapes a curvaceous 5' 4" frame fit for a woman half her age. Looks truly *can* be deceiving! Once this geriatric beauty opens her mouth, all dignity is thrust aside! Don't let the gray hairs fool you! She is in no way fragile, and the infinite filth that escapes her soul by way of tongue will definitely make you want to break her! This old bitty doesn't need to be taught any new tricks because the one she used to get Adam and Eve kicked out of the Garden still works to this day!

I have lots of cousins here too, so family is everywhere. That being the case, why was I so alone? Well, I've learned that a family is only as good as its roots, and my family's roots seem to bring forth weeds.

I've been clean and sober for eight years now. It wasn't easy to break off my friendship with the bottle, but it was definitely doable. It was more a struggle, though, because my husband Walter would not go through the process with me. He's still a heavy drinker, and this continues to create conflict in our marriage. He liked when I drank…not because that meant he'd have a drinking buddy, but because my drinking kept me oblivious to his philandering. We would go to the club and dance, laugh, and drink. He just kept them coming, round after round. He would have a couple of drinks, but most of them were for me. We were not husband and wife at the time, but we were together and having fun. Whenever he saw that I could no longer walk without tripping over my own toenails, he would take me home. After tucking me in, he would go back to the club to continue the evening without me. Sometimes in my drunken slumber I'd think, "It's nice-a-him to get me home safe!" This thought would cause my heart to swell with happiness and I'd yell out, "I got me a good man and can't none-a-dem bitches have him…not even his wife!" He was mine, and he was taking good care of me.

My, how times have changed. As I sit here reflecting on the different phases our relationship has gone through up to this point, I realize that – somehow—I've been down this road before. No two situations were exactly the same. This was a different man and a different time, but everything else was just all too familiar to me. It's like déjà vu. Walter is every man that has ever meant anything to me. There are so many similarities. Where do I begin?

CHAPTER TWO

Reverend Matthew Prays for the Naked

I *would* start with my eldest child's father, but there was no relationship at all. He was a friend of the family, and when opportunity presented itself he took from me that which I was not willing to give to him. Nine months later, my daughter Janice was born. I hated to look at her because I'd see his face. I didn't even want to hold her. That lack of bonding is still evident today. She hates me so much. She grew up with a deep hatred for me within her. As a child, she was so defiant. I remember her not wanting to eat dinner one night because she wanted to eat sweets instead. That girl would not eat no matter how much I threatened her! Finally, I took a spoon and started shoveling food into her mouth myself! You know what she did? She held that food in her cheeks like a squirrel until the next day, which was when I finally told her to spit it out. By then, the food smelled very foul because it had spoiled. That's the type of child Janice was. Even then, she would look at me as if she were secretly plotting my demise. I would see the look in her eyes and then try to smack the devil out of her. This stubborn minion wouldn't even cry. She would just stare me down with the most evil stare. Every time she challenged me in this manner, my trusty extension cord would break her. It would break her skin. It would break her spirits. Little girls *do* cry and she would be reminded that she *was* a little girl after all.

I couldn't start by telling you about my son Matt's father either. I remember taking a Greyhound bus out of state one time and seeing this man a few seats away from me. He was light-skinned…possibly Hispanic. I thought, "Wow! I think that's Matt's father!" Maybe it was. Maybe it wasn't. I'll never know for sure.

I'll start with Matthew. Matthew was my first boyfriend. We'd known each other since childhood in North Carolina. Even when we grew apart, he still had a place in my heart. That's why I gave my firstborn son his name. When our paths crossed a second time, he chose to be with me even though I had two children by two other men. It was a wonderful feeling.

Fall of 1971 found Matthew, my two children, and myself living in a hotel in New York. We both found jobs, but by the end of the summer of 1972 I had to stop working because I was nearing the end of my pregnancy with Matthew's daughter. At that point, Matthew allowed me to handle the finances in order to help me feel that I was still doing my part. As the money came in, I took care of everything. I paid all of the bills, went grocery shopping, and lugged our laundry to the laundromat. If any of our clothing became damaged or too worn, I would replace them without him noticing the old ones had been thrown away. After all the bills were paid and we were all clothed and fed, I made sure I put a nice sum of money in the bank like I did when I was working. Every week, I would make a nice deposit. I wanted to make sure that we would be prepared if anything came up. I couldn't work, but I was still an active participant in this relationship. I felt good about that.

After my chores were done, my days would mostly

be spent in the park with the children. They always loved to go to the park, so I would pack us a nice lunch and take them to their playground. Matt was the baby, so he got every little thing we could give him. On our way to the park, someone would always be selling little toys on the street, so every day I would end up getting Matt something different. He was so happy. There wasn't much that Janice wanted. At home, she was content playing grown-up. She loved pocketbooks and makeup. She even played mother to her dolls by yelling at them, banging them together, and throwing them across the room. At the park, she would just kind of run off and play by herself. Occasionally, she would get with the other kids so she could trip them as they ran about or push them head first down the sliding board. She was such a malevolent child, but she was my little monster.

My parents were still in North Carolina, and my father had been sick off and on for a while. Whenever he was in really bad shape, I would go to be with him. Matthew always encouraged me to be by my father's side, and I thought that was sweet. He never went with me, though. Neither of my sisters up here would go either because they didn't want to leave their men. Each time daddy got sick, I would take my kids to North Carolina and we'd stay about a week. Then, he'd get a little better and the kids and I would return to New York.

In early August, my mother called and told me that my father died. She said he had passed away a few minutes ago. I didn't hear her voice anymore, so I thought she had hung up the phone. Meanwhile, she thought that I had fainted at the news and she didn't know what to say or do. After a long silence, I managed to tell her that I'd be leaving first thing in the morning.

When I got off the phone, I told Matthew of my father's death and that I was gonna leave with the kids in the morning. Matthew then went to my sisters' homes to give them the bad news personally because neither of the two had a phone.

In the morning, the kids and I were once again on

the bus to North Carolina. My sisters would begin their trip in the evening. When the kids and I reached our destination, I was told that I could go to the funeral but I was not to view the body. On top of that, I had forgotten that the family had a plot in Georgia; that was where my father was going to be buried. This meant that I could not attend the burial because I was already due to have my third child. All wasn't lost, though. A lot of us just stayed in North Carolina with all of the smaller children until my mother returned from her husband's burial. When she *did* return, she brought with her my aunts, uncles, and a couple of boys that were in college with my African brother…or was he my cousin? Everyone stayed for a few days and then went on to Elizabeth City. It was still too risky for me to travel anywhere, so September crept up on me before I had ever realized it. I was bigger than ever, so I couldn't wobble that far even if I wanted to.

Since I had been away from my Matthew for awhile now, I walked to the pay phone to give him a call. I needed to let him know that I wouldn't be able to come home yet because I wasn't allowed to ride the bus at this stage of pregnancy. After three rings, a woman answered my phone and told me that he had not gotten home from work yet. I hung up thinking, "What just happened here?" Somehow, I managed to keep my cool and returned an hour later to give it another try. This time, I could hear *a lot* of women in the background. The woman that answered the phone said they were having a prayer meeting with "Reverend Matthew". I said I wanted to speak to him *anyway*, so the woman passed the phone to him. At first, the tone of his greeting was pleasant because he didn't know *who* was calling…he only knew that a *woman* was on the line. I asked him what was going on there and why that woman was calling him "Reverend Matthew". Upon recognizing my voice, he wasn't loud, but his voice grew cold. "What do ya want?" he asked. I responded, "Well, I *was* calling to tell you that they won't let me get on the bus until after the baby is born, but what *I* wanna know is what the *hell* is goin' on up there? Why is some *bitch* answering my phone, and why is she calling you 'Reverend Matthew'?" This Demon of Righteousness muttered, "I don't *want* you to come back...not now, and not after the baby is born!" That did it! I called him every foul word known to man and a few that I made up on the spot! I was so busy fussin' and cussin' that I didn't realize I was talking to dial tone. Every time I tried to call him after that, the line was busy. I was *furious*, so I stormed back to my mother's house to vent.

Now that daddy was dead, my mother had so-called friends coming out of the woodwork. Thanks to her constant blabbing, everyone knew she'd be getting some money so they wanted to be there to get their share. They were all using her. They always needed money or were always in need of something that cost a lot of it. To keep from appearing so obviously greedy, some came to "borrow" money, though they had no intentions of paying it back.

The one friend in particular that stands out in my mind is my mother's best friend Betsy Mae. Each day when I was either in the yard or on the front porch,

Betsy Mae and her son Billy, would come around. The first couple of days, they would make light conversation and pretend to be checking up on the grieving widow. After that, Betsy Mae was always asking my mother to let her "hold something" until she got her next check. Billy would talk to me more and more with each visit, and he even started bringing me things. He was cute, so I didn't mind the attention. Both of our mothers could see his interest in me, and they encouraged me to date him. After Billy and his mother would leave, my mother would talk about him like a dog and tell me that she didn't want me dating him. "He's a no-good bastard!" she would say. "He done got so he comes over here *without* his mother now! I *know* he's only comin' to see *you*! Ya see how he be kissin' on yo sista's baby all the time? He acts like that's *his* young 'un! His cousin is supposed to be the child's daddy, but *he* spend mo' time with the baby than the daddy does! I think that young 'un is his! I told him before! I said, 'If it ain't yo young 'un, you should stop making it look like it is 'cause even ya own mammy is startin' to think that's yo baby!' You stay away from that boy, 'cause he ain't no good!"

I didn't think that was a good enough reason for her to dislike him so much, so I really didn't know why my mother felt the way she did about Billy. It seemed to me that he loved children, though I had no idea at the time that the only child he would give his attention to was my sister's baby. I thought he was a nice guy, so I made a date to go out with him in spite of my mother's disapproval. I got ready and then heard him knocking at the door. As soon as he knocked, my water broke. I *should* have taken that as a sign, but I wasn't thinking. Instead, I simply told him I was feeling sick and that we'd have to go out another time. After convincing him to leave, I told my mother my water broke and I needed to go to the hospital. My mother took me to the hospital, and my third child, Melody, was born. The next day, Billy came to see me and asked why I waited until he left to tell my mother I needed to go to the hospital. He said he had wanted to be with me when the baby was born. I *knew* he was a nice guy!

Upon leaving the hospital the day after Melody's birth, I decided that I was going back to New York because that was more *my* home than Matthew's. Two weeks later, my children and I were on the bus. On the way to New York I had a change of heart and decided that Matthew could keep the place. I would just gather my things and the children's things and move back to North Carolina. When I made it to my New York home, Matthew was not there so I cleaned up the place in between packing and tending to the kids. While cleaning up, I found nude pictures that Matthew had taken of a lot of girls. I also found letters on top of letters from young girls saying that they were in love with him. They said that whenever they would come over and he would pray for them, they loved him even more. In eight of the letters I read, the girls said they were pregnant with his child. This was unbelievable! I read as many of the letters as I could and still never got to *a third* of them. I tried to process all of this new information, but my mind was overloaded. Some of the dates on the letters went as far back as two months after we had moved to New

York. I started thinking that many times when he told me he was at work, he was actually at someone's house preying...I mean *praying*. My thoughts were running wild until I heard a knock at the door. I wasn't ready for any of this, and I definitely wasn't ready for what awaited me on the other side of that door. It was a young girl coming to see "Reverend Matthew". I let her in 'cause she looked as if she were ready to have *her* baby at any moment. I felt bad, but more for her than for myself. We talked. She told me that her name was Faye and that she was fifteen years old. She said she was always doing something that she wasn't supposed to be doing, so one day her mother introduced her to "Reverend Matthew" in hopes that he could talk to her about her behavior and pray for her. At first, Faye wouldn't talk to him at all, so he told her mother he and Faye would need privacy because he felt she wouldn't open up to him with her mother around. He vowed that if he could just talk to Faye and pray for her behind closed doors he would make a breakthrough and her daughter's life would be changed forever. Faye's mother agreed and allowed him to counsel Faye in the girl's bedroom with the door locked as reassurance that she wouldn't interfere...after all, he *was* a man of the cloth, so what could *possibly* happen? She would go about her daily chores and sometimes even go grocery shopping while Matthew was in the bedroom taking sexual liberties with her daughter.

Faye said that the first time she and "Reverend Matthew" were alone in her room, she didn't want him touching her. She resisted, but his talking calmed her. He said all the right things to make her feel like he cared about her and wanted to help her. He said her mother didn't understand her but *he* knew she was misbehaving because she was feeling so bad on the inside. He said he knew how to make her feel good. Her pregnancy became visible after a few months, and her mother was *furious*. She was even more upset after learning who the baby's father was. At that point, she decided to have a talk with "Reverend Matthew". He smooth talked her too. Ultimately, he said he wanted to help and he wanted to take care of Faye, so Faye's mother told him the apartment across the hall from hers was vacant. She said he and Faye should live there. He thought it was a great idea, so Faye's mother talked to the superintendent about it. As soon as the apartment had been cleaned, Faye and "Reverend Matthew" moved into it. He had told Faye that he was still going to hold onto the place he already had 'cause that was where he held his group prayer meetings. She hadn't seen him much since they moved in together. That was why she came knocking.

Faye was visibly hurting, and with good reason. When she saw my newborn, she couldn't help but break down. I told her about my relationship with Matthew and about the pictures and letters I had just found. She flipped through the pictures and found that some were strangers but others were either friends of hers or girls from her school. When she flipped through the letters, she found that one of them was from her mother. In that letter, her mother expressed how angry she was that Matthew was having sex with *her* but messing with her daughter behind her back. She said that she never for once thought that he would make a move on her daughter…especially since he'd spoken of counseling others like Faye who were merely "lost, little girls in need of a father figure". She said that she trusted him to help improve her daughter's situation, but he'd only made it worse. All things considered, she was still drawn to him because she enjoyed the sex. She went on to say that the only reason she wanted Matthew and Faye to stay across the hall from her was to make it easy for the two of *them* to get together. Mother Dear said that since she did things with him that her daughter could never *dream* of, she knew he would be coming back for more. She praised him for lying with her when her daughter thought he was at work, and she vowed to only get freakier as time went on because she liked the idea of "turning out" a Reverend.

This girl's heart was broken badly at fifteen…once by a self-proclaimed reverend and once by the now thirty-year-old woman who brought her into this world. Matthew had said that if he could talk to Faye behind closed doors he could change her life forever.

Well, that's *one* thing he didn't lie about. I left a very hurt little girl in New York, but I had to get on with *my* life.

CHAPTER THREE

Don't Bank On It

When the children and I returned to North Carolina, the weather had gotten *so* cold. We stayed with my mother, although she wasn't home that much. She was still spending daddy's dough. When she first got the money, she told me that she was going to give me some for the two kids and the one that was on the way. She said it would only be a hundred dollars apiece, but she would open an account for us and put the money in it. That was the first and last time I've heard anything about that. She never gave us any money, but she did take care of the men in her life. She bought a barbershop for one guy and a club for another...at least she had her priorities straight.

Billy and I picked up from where we'd left off. We started getting really close. My mother still was against it and threatened to put me out of the house if I continued to go out with him. My sister Brandee told me that my mother didn't want me to move back to North Carolina because my mother was messing with

Billy and had been since before I had ever met him. I didn't believe her, so I continued seeing Billy. Don't mistake me for a fool, though...I started searching for a place of my own as I continued to see Billy. My mother was so upset over my defiance that she called Matthew. I don't know what it was that she told him. Of course, I didn't even know at the time that she *had* called him.

Night was drawing near, and at that time of day my mother would send one of us outside to get her night pot. A night pot was a plastic bucket that had a lid. It was a lot like the buckets that large amounts of paint are sold in, and some folks kept one in their bedrooms just in case they had to go to the bathroom during the night. After all, who'd want to get up late at night, unlock the back door to the house, and go to the back porch to use the bathroom? A lot of times, it was just too cold for that...especially when wearing pajamas! People would use the night pot at night and flush its contents down the toilet in the morning. Most people kept the pot outside during the day because daily use resulted in a stench that would fill the house even with the lid on after a good cleaning. I don't know who came up with such a funky idea. I'd choose the cold over the stench of a night pot any day! Nonetheless, a couple of nights after my mother called Matthew and said whatever it was that she said to him, she sent me outside to get her night pot. When I got out there, Matthew grabbed me. He was yelling and hitting and even tried to throw me down the well. Since my mother was the only adult in the house at the time, I called her. I was screaming for her, but I guess she didn't hear me. When I finally managed to get away, I ran into the house and told her he was beating on me. She showed no sign of interest. I knew I was on my own, so I ran into the kitchen and got a knife. I waited with my back to a wall until sunrise. Later the next day, he showed up again. He wouldn't come near me, though, because my sister and her boyfriend were there. Matthew just hung around Farmville for a little while and then went back to New York.

A few days later, it suddenly dawned on me that when I left New York I'd forgotten to close my bank

account. I called the bank and was told I'd have to
come down there and that Matthew had to come too
since the account was in both of our names. How do
I get a man who'd just tried to throw me down a well
to cooperate? I hadn't a clue. I guess I was just young
and stupid because I made a trip to New York in spite
of everything in order to tie up this loose end. I went
to see Matthew and told him why I was there and
what the bank had told me. He said there wasn't any
money in the account because—during a long period
of time that he was out of work—while we were
together, he would withdraw what amounted to a
week's pay and bring it home to me so I would think
he was still working. I told him that if *I* can't
withdraw money without *him* then *he* couldn't
withdraw any without *me*. This big, fat Zero told me
that he had gotten one of his lady friends to say she
was me, and they took until there wasn't anything left
to take. He taunted, "Go ahead! Call the bank and ask
them for your balance if you don't believe me!" Well,
I wasn't gonna take a liar's word for it, so I made the
call. It was true; the account had a zero balance.

You'd think the representative I'd spoken with before leaving North Carolina would have told me this or would have just closed the account by phone since no money was going to exchange hands! When I found out there was no money in the account, I explained the situation to the rep but was told there wasn't anything that could be done about it.

When I remembered the New York bank account, I should have just counted it as a loss and moved on. Now, I'd have to fight to leave because Matthew said he wasn't going to let me go back to North Carolina. Luckily, I expected him to try to beat on me again, so I had told my sister Carol and her boyfriend—who happens to be Matthew's brother—to meet me at Matthew's place. Their timing was perfect. Once he let them in, I told them about the bank account and said there was no reason for me to be in New York since the account was empty. I told them I wanted to leave but Matthew wouldn't let me. My sister called me a cab while her boyfriend tried to talk to Matthew. When the cab arrived, Matthew tried to stop me from leaving. He seemed to think he could beat me up to make me stay. He thought I was afraid of him, but I had made up my mind to be done with him for good. When he started hitting me, I fought him like a mad tiger! My sister jumped in, and we beat the hell out of him! Her boyfriend tried to break it up, but he never hit us in the process. When I grabbed my bag and headed for the door, Matthew came after me again...I guess he was a glutton for punishment. This time, his brother grabbed him, pinned him to the floor, and told me to call when my bus was about to leave. He said he was gonna keep Matthew with him at all times until he was sure I was gone. I took the taxi to the bus station and called right before boarding the bus. I could finally close this chapter of my life and hope for better days.

CHAPTER FOUR

Keep It In The Family

Now, I was back in North Carolina for good. At this time, it looked like a Christmas postcard. There was quite a bit of snow on the ground, and the snow was still falling slowly. Billy and I resumed dating, but my mother still protested. It didn't take her long to give me an ultimatum: "Stop seeing him or leave!" I told this mother of mine that I was a grown woman and could run my own life. I *refused* to stop seeing Billy. After all, it was *my* life and *my* choice. My seeing Billy was none of her business and had nothing to do with her. Nothing she could say could make me feel like I was wrong about this. She would just have to accept that I was my own woman.

In my heart, I was right…but in this world, I was homeless. I wasn't alone, though. My year-old son Matt was with me. My mother put him out but kept the other two kids. I guess that was because Matt was light-skinned and the other two were darker like her. Matt had neither coat nor shoes. What kind of woman would take her anger out on an innocent child? *He* wasn't dating Billy. *I* was.

Since I still hadn't found a place of my own, I figured I'd go to Billy's house. His house was way across town. I could have walked *through* town, but the trip would have taken just as long as walking on the outskirts. Plus, there were a lot of dogs in town, and I didn't need the added stress. I put my poor baby's feet in the top of my pants, zipped him up inside my jacket so we were belly to belly, and started my journey. I was so afraid that my baby's feet were gonna get frostbite, so I moved as fast as I could. The snow was deep but more so because my frame only spanned four feet ten inches. It was such a struggle. At one point, I wanted to give up and try to make it back to my mother's house, but my pride wouldn't let me. I 'd finally reached the road that led to the houses in the country. This meant I had two miles to go. I knew that would be the longest, darkest, coldest walk I would ever take. I pressed on. Every time I saw a car's headlights, I would get off the road and hide in the woods until the car had passed because I didn't want some stranger taking advantage of my harsh reality. I only hid a couple of times before finally reaching Billy's house.

Betsy Mae greeted us at the door. I told her my mother put us out. She too found it hard to understand my mother's reasoning. Nonetheless, she fed Matt and put him to bed. She then gave me her bedroom right before saying, "Billy, say goodnight, now, 'cause I better not see you tiptoeing by moonlight to get to her! Ain't *nobody* gone be havin' no relations up in *here*! I'm gone be right in that there livin' room, and I'm a light sleeper!" We said goodnight, and finally I could rest.

The next day, Billy took me to get my other two kids and then to Greenville to find a place of my own. He thought it would be a good idea for me to go to Human Resources Services, so we went *there* first. I told a caseworker my situation and that my kids and I needed a place to stay. The caseworker told me that since I was only nineteen, I *had* to stay with my mother. That hit me like a fist to the solar plexus. A couple of HRS representatives then took me and the kids *back* to my mother's house. They thought they could talk her into letting me stay, but she wasn't budging. "But, Mrs. Woods," said the first rep, "your daughter is only nineteen, *and* she has three children. She has no place to live, and your grandchildren are on the streets *with* her! I *know* you don't want your grandbabies on the streets! You've *gotta* let her back in!" My mother took a couple more puffs from her cigarette before replying, "Well, I'll kiss *my own ass*! How the *hell* you gone tell me I *gotta* let somebody live in *my* house?!? I ain't gotta do shit! Get cha ass off my land!" Her refusal was music to my ears.

Unhappy with having to make a meal of their own words, the HRS reps took us back to Greenville and then to a small apartment not far from their office. The place was already furnished, but all of the furniture was piled up and in need of being arranged in a manner suitable for living. The reps gave me a check and some food stamps and said someone would be working with me to help me get on my feet.

Billy brought me food and cleaning supplies. For two weeks, our days consisted of tending to the children and fixing up the apartment. He was so helpful. He never spent the night, but he would come over very early in the morning and leave very late at night. By the end of the second week, the apartment was so clean and neatly arranged that I was glad to call it home. As I basked in the fruits of my labor and watched the children play with their toys, a new feeling took over me. It was that of freedom. I was free, and it felt good.

Now that my home was in order, Billy would come by to take the kids and I to his house so the kids could play with other children that lived nearby. I had always gotten a loving, caring vibe from Betsy Mae, but not anymore. She was still friends with my mother, so I figured that my mother must have filled her head with lies and turned her against me. She seemed to hate me now, but since Billy told me he'd be leaving for the Army tomorrow and couldn't come home for a visit until six weeks later, I knew she and I wouldn't be seeing much of each other anymore. I just let it go.

While Billy was gone, I made another friend, and he was teaching me to drive. I didn't know that his mother and my mother were friends too. This gave my mother ammo and Betsy Mae an even better reason to hate me. When Billy finally *was* able to come home for a visit, his mother told him I was messing around with another guy. She and my mother talked him into a fury and told him he should "knock some sense into" my head—literally. My mother knew that if Billy were to hit me, I wouldn't want to be with him anymore; she would finally get what she wanted. Billy showed up to take me out but instead took me into the woods and jumped on me. In between blows, he would recite the lines that he'd been fed. I couldn't convince him that they were lying. After all, one was his mother and the other was his lover. I didn't know this at first, nor did I believe it when my sister Brandee first told me. All I know is that ever since Billy and I broke up, I'd seen a car that looked a lot like my mother's parked in the same spot in the woods every night that he was in town.One night, Brandee and I wanted to know who was doing all that sneaking around, so we walked up to the car and looked inside. I was shocked, but it was old news to Brandee. She said she had always known and that was why she had stopped Billy from hanging around her and her baby. Everything made sense now. I thought Billy was a nice guy, but he was no different than the previous men in my life. This Demon of Stealth showed me *exactly* what he wanted me to see. As for my mother…you know, I don't even know what to say about her.

CHAPTER FIVE

Craig the Jackal...Tony the Nut

Upon getting on with my life, I met a guy in Greenville named Craig, and he soon moved in with me. Everyone called him "Junior". He was eighteen. When I first started seeing him, he had a fourteen-year-old girlfriend named Mary and a fifteen-year-old one named Nadine. Mary was only about three inches taller than me, and in that blue dress she often wore, she looked like nighttime over the Pacific. Although her hair was really short, she always managed to pull it back into an almond of a ponytail. She certainly didn't seem like Craig's type—or anybody's, for that matter. Nadine was the anti-Mary. She was one of those red-boned girls that the guys go crazy over. She was about five inches taller than Mary, very shapely, and had light brown hair that massaged her shoulders constantly. Lula Mae, Nadine's thirty-five-year-old mother, was Craig's other woman. Nadine was a carbon copy of her [though Lula Mae's curves were a little fuller than her daughter's].

I didn't know that Craig had these girlfriends at

the time. Well, the word on the streets was that he was seeing Nadine, but I thought he had broken up with her. While Nadine's father was at work, he didn't want Craig around his house, so he told Craig to stay away from her. In actuality, Craig wasn't going with Nadine at all. They were pretending so that he could be with her mother. You see, Nadine's father was about fifteen years older than her mother, and he kept a tight leash on both of them. He was so militant that his wife and daughter were practically prisoners in the three-bedroom ranch that they called home. Lula Mae promised not to have company visit her but managed to convince her husband that their daughter needed to socialize in order to fit in. She swayed him to allow Nadine's friends to visit, saying that if they hung out at the house they wouldn't be "out there" getting into trouble or doing things that teenagers ought not be doing. Nadine's father agreed but wouldn't budge when it came to Craig. He said Craig should be *working* during business hours instead of visiting Nadine. While her husband was on the job, Lula Mae allowed Nadine to go wherever she wanted and do whatever she wanted. As far as Nadine's father could see, Craig was no longer visiting his home. As far as outsiders could see, Craig was there to visit his young girlfriend. To Nadine, Craig was a ticket to freedom. To Lula Mae, Craig was the dim light that lit her cell each day until the warden could flip the switch. Mother and daughter did and said whatever was necessary in order to protect their alliance and guard their secret.

Lula Mae must have really loved Craig to risk everything for the sake of being with him. Since Mary and Nadine attended the same school, Lula Mae found out that Craig was seeing Mary, but she didn't feel threatened because---when she confronted him about it—he'd told her that it was platonic. She wanted him so badly that when she found out he and *I* were seeing each other and that I was having his baby, she came over and told me everything. She even asked me what I would do if I could catch him in the act. At first, I thought it wasn't worth it and she could just have him. Then, I decided that she could *still* have him, but I wanted him to know that I knew what was going on. I told her to tell him that her husband was home so they should meet in the park. Once everything was in the open, Lula Mae wanted Craig all to herself. This prompted her to have Nadine talk to Mary and let her in on the plan. An angry Mary agreed to be there with me out of sight but within earshot…and so it was.

Lula Mae sat on a bench in the park and waited for Craig. Mary and I entered the park through a rear entrance just in case Craig was home looking out for Lula Mae through a window. We knelt behind a row of bushes to her rear right. The park's entrance was ahead and to the left, so we knew Craig wouldn't see the two of us hiding behind bushes that I could barely see over when standing. We could see him coming, though, because his family's house was directly across an open meadow that stood between their home and the entrance to the park. When Craig arrived, he fondled and kissed Lula Mae while asking if they were gonna "do it" on the bench or in the grass. She reluctantly pushed him away and told him she knew the truth about me and Mary so he needed to choose

which of us he wanted. "I'm here with *you*, ain't I?"
Craig began. "I wanna be with *you*, but I can't 'cause
you have a husband. I have to watch your house most
of the time to see when he comes and when he goes
just so I could spend some time with you. Mary is just
my *ex* girlfriend. I told you before! We ain't messin'
around or nothin'. I go over there and sit with her
sometimes just to please my people. Her family is
friends with mine, and both families think we would
be a good couple. They want us to be together. That's
why I started seeing her in the first place. She's a nice
girl, but she's not for me. We sit and talk, but that's it.
Like I said before, it's strictly platonic. I'm not
attracted to her at all, but I thought that if I played
along, no one would be suspicious of me and you."
"Well, what about Gerri?" Lula Mae demanded.
"They said you and her are living together and that
she's having your baby! What about that?" "People
think they know my business, but they don't!" Craig
responded. "I ain't with Gerri 'cause my people can't
stand her! I heard that she's pregnant, too, but half
this county could be that baby's daddy! You're the

one I want, but I gotta either wait or pretend I'm coming over to see your daughter to get next to you. I don't like it any more than you do. If you ask me, *you're* the one that needs to choose!"

Mary and I stepped out of hiding. Once Craig saw us, he found himself face up on the ground before he could even *think* about running. "If we're fuckin', it ain't platonic!" Mary yelled before introducing her knee to Craig's nuts. We tore him up! His family could see us whippin' on him from a distance, and they tried to make it there to help him. Unfortunately for him, there was no help for that ass that evening! When we were finished with him, his pants were torn as if a cat got hold of him. I was satisfied. I got pleasure out of seeing him make a fool of himself. I knew that *I* had more power over him than the other two, and he proved it by begging me to stay with him as I turned and walked away. By then, his family was there fussin' and cussin'. They tried to get in my face and got mad when he shielded me from them. He was protecting me, but it was still the end of the line for us.

When I moved out of the home I shared with Craig, I went back to New York and got a place of my own. Once again, I worked close to time for my baby to be born. Craig wanted to be there for the birth, so I allowed him to come stay with me. I still couldn't stand him, but if he wanted to be with his son, I wanted to give him that much respect. My boyfriend at the time didn't like that I wouldn't go out with him or call him anymore. Once he found out Craig was staying with me, he chose to go his separate way.

Craig was strange. At night, he would stare at me as I slept, and if I opened my eyes, he'd jump and race out of the room. I would make a mental note of how strangely he looked at me, and the next day I would ask him about his behavior. It was of no use, though, because he would pretend he didn't know what I was talking about. He could pretend, but I'll always remember him staring at me as if I were a creature of unknown origin.

Once Craig, Jr. was born, I went back to work.

Though his stay was supposed to be brief, Craig was already working but would always be home sitting in a room with one of my friends whenever I got home. Each time, the friend would say that she came to see *me,* but it was a lie because once I was home, she was ready to leave. Craig said he was now working nights because he made a little more money that way. I was so into my job and making money that I really didn't care what he did.

One night after Craig left for work, I went to visit one of my friends to talk to her about being at my place when I wasn't home. When she let me into her home, Craig could not explain why he was at her place instead of at work. My friend said he had stopped by to see her husband and she was just telling him that her husband works nights now so he'd have to catch up with him earlier in the day. Craig took that as his cue to leave and said he was on his way to work anyway, so he should go. It seemed innocent, so I really thought he had stopped by to see her husband as she had said. After shootin' the breeze with her for a little bit, I went to the house of my other friend that was often at my place whenever I wasn't home. She had told me earlier that she wanted to talk, so I figured now was the time.Not long after I arrived at her place, Craig showed up. He didn't know I was in the next room, so he entered her home groping and kissing her like he did Lula Mae at the park. I guess my friend had decided to let his actions say to me what she couldn't. While he groped her, he said he had told me he was working nights. This Demon of Deception went on to say that in a way he wasn't lying because spending nights with her *was* a lot of work. She asked if he had worked the other night when he *didn't* come over, and his answer was yes. As she walked toward the room I was in, she told him that she had followed him that night and saw him go to another girl's house. Before he could utter his next lie, we three were in the same room. My friend looked at me, as did Craig. She asked me if I was hurt or disappointed. I said that in North Carolina we beat him up for the same crap and ever since, I couldn't get myself to feel anything for him...not even when he would touch me. I was neither hurt nor disappointed by his actions because I wasn't into him. "However," I continued, "this so-called friendship is over!"

Now that I had removed a little scum from my life, my next task was to get a *lot* of scum out of my home. My sister Wilmer started coming over a lot with her boyfriend Mark. Their presence complicated matters for me. They never asked to stay at my place; they just started staying. Mark was a friend of Craig's from North Carolina, so the two of them were having the time of their lives. I was paying all of the bills, and Mark and Craig were going around doing whatever the hell they wanted. They had to go. Craig should have been out of the door *already,* but I was too embarrassed to let my sister know that he had played me yet again. At this point, though, the men were behaving like juveniles, and we women were tired of them. I told them that I wanted them out. At first they ignored me, but then they plotted to agree to leave upon my giving them bus fare to North Carolina. They'd planned to use the money to party and buy sneakers, and then they would laugh in my face. Fortunately, Mark's mouth was bigger than his ego, so it didn't take long for their plan to get back to me. When they approached me for bus fare, I handed both of them a ticket to North Carolina...checkmate! I left the three of them at my place and went to stay in a hotel. My sister Carol kept my children, so it was easy for me to lay low at the hotel until my apartment had been vacated. Eventually, the three of them had no choice but to leave because the utilities were being shut off at my request. Once out of my place, Mark and Craig had no place to go. They made their way back to North Carolina, and Wilmer went to stay with my sister that was keeping my kids. Craig was finally out of my life for good, so I moved on.

After Craig, I met a guy named Tony. He's hardly worth mentioning, though. I never figured him out. We went out for six months. During that time, he took me to the park, to museums, and to dinner at nice restaurants. He was very polite and didn't mind wining and dining me. He never tried *anything* with me, though...know what I mean? We went to his place lots of times, but he never even tried to kiss me.

It's like he was content with being with me and enjoying my company. He never seemed to want anything else from me no matter how much I hinted at wanting something else from him: I wore short skirts and bent over in front of him a lot; I always made sure that my cleavage was visible regardless of the weather conditions; and I would casually touch him in a sensual manner whenever we were together. I got nothing! How could you date a person for six months and not try to get sex? Six months and no sex...what was the purpose? Was he a man, or what? What planet was he from? I *know* he wasn't from my world. I just couldn't figure this guy out, and I didn't want to. What I wanted to do was have sex, so I dumped this Demon of Morality and started dating a friend of his. Six months without sex...what kind of girl did he think I was?!? Thanks to him, I had a lot of catching up to do.

CHAPTER SIX

The Devil's Playground

I keep having this dream that a man is looking for me, and when he finds me he's going to kill me. I keep dreaming that this guy is everywhere I go. He's someone I once knew, and it's been years since I last saw him or even heard his name mentioned. I last saw this guy, JD, in 1978 when the police were looking for him. He was a junkie and would kill his mother to get whatever it was he wanted.

A friend of mine told me that JD once crashed a wedding party his mother was throwing for one of his sisters. She said that about ninety-nine guests other than herself were gathered at the ranch home of one of JD's uncles, and it was obvious that his mother had gone all out in preparation. Everyone was dressed formally and ready to toast the bride and groom when JD and some other guys walked in with knives and baseball bats in hand. They terrorized the party guests, smashing things with their bats and then robbing everyone at knife point. No one dared make a stand because everyone there knew JD or at least knew *of* him. They knew of his ruthless beatings of others and of his junkie mentality. They also knew that he sometimes carried a gun. The only reason anyone agreed to attend the party was because no one had seen him in a while and word spread that he'd been locked up. But, there he was…reaching down his mother's blouse to snatch her gold necklace by the cross that hung between her breasts. No one at the party dared to call the police for fear of waking up dead.

I didn't know *that* JD at the time. I didn't know that his mother was so afraid of him that she would help him get his dope in order to keep him from beating on her and her man. She would sell her furniture or anything else that she *could* so as to appease the savage beast that she'd spawned.

Now that I know what I know, I'd have to say that JD's behavior had its roots in his mother's teachings. I don't know what happened in her past to make her teach her children the things that she did, but those details might be too much for me to handle anyway.

I mean, what would make a woman teach her sons that the perfect women to bed are aged four to a hundred? Where would she get something like that, and why would she pass it on to her kids?

She didn't steer her daughters in the right direction, either. One of her daughters, Estrella, was also a dope fiend and was married to a really nice, older white man named Jake. Estrella would steal Jake's wallet and disappear for days at a time, but that wasn't the worst of it. Sometimes, she would bring another man into their one bedroom apartment and start putting the moves on him right in front of her husband. If her husband protested or tried to leave, she and her dope fiend boy toy would beat on him till he could hardly move. Then, they would have sex as her husband's blood trickled to the floor. After the linen absorbed the last few drops of sweat, Estrella would take Jake's money and disappear again. Finally, Jake got tired of this and left her. At that point, Estrella got her mother to call him and tell him that she was sorry and wanted him to forgive her and come back. She knew that he would come back because he loved her. He loved her because she was half his age. Jake agreed to speak with Estrella, and—after doing so—he agreed to pick her up. When he showed up at his mother-in-law's home to retrieve his wife, his wife began to seduce him with her words. She hugged him and touched him and told him she wanted to stay in a hotel room...one with a really big bed. She said that if they were in a really big bed, she could open her legs *real* wide. Jake must have been picturing his slender, buxom Latina beauty in such a pose because her words excited him, and he quickly forgot that his beloved, young wife was the devil in disguise. He didn't wonder why she wanted him to go, check into a hotel room, and *then* come back for her. My guess is that there just wasn't enough blood left in his brain. He just went to the hotel. He couldn't check in, though, because his wallet was no longer in his jacket pocket. When he realized that she had done it again, Jake headed back to his mother-in-law's home. He didn't know that as soon as he'd left for the hotel, Estrella went through his new, leather wallet and split his money with her mother. Estrella then took the credit cards for herself and threw the wallet away. She had instructed her mother to pretend to be crushed by what she had done and by her disappearance. When Jake reached the home and banged on the door, Estrella's mother poured on the waterworks. "I just don't know what's wrong with her!" she sobbed. "Why does she keep doing stuff like this? I tried to stop her, but there was nothing I could do. Why would she make her mother feel this way? Why? She wouldn't even say where she was going. She just left. She needs help. Oh, Lord, have mercy!" She cried to the Lord, and then she cried with Jake.

At the time, JD and Estrella's mother was forty-seven. She always looked very young and dressed nicely. She was as tall as professional models usually are…I guess that's where JD got his height. She looked like one of those women from the soap operas on tv. You know, the ones with long hair, clear skin, and a figure that appeared to know neither donut nor childbearing. She was beautiful on the outside, but hideous within. All was well, and during these good times she taught her children to mistreat their mates. She condoned their behavior whenever they were doing wrong. If one of her children went to her for advice about a disagreement with a mate, she'd say, "A good ass-whippin' would solve everything!" I bet she never expected to be on the receiving end when her children's battered mates could take it no longer and went their separate ways. Once JD turned to her to take the place of the last woman he'd beaten and stolen from, his mother's frustrations began to take a physical toll on her. She started looking much older than she actually was because her hair started falling out and her skin dried to a wrinkle. That shapely figure of hers lost all its plumpness, and she lived in fear of this horrible man whose evil roots were embedded in her womb.

Like I said, I didn't know *that* JD in the beginning. The JD I knew was tall and good-looking...a suave Rican.The patch he wore over his left eye made him all the sexier. The streets knew him, and he knew the streets. He had this magnetism about him that made women want him. Some of them had good husbands and good homes, but if they saw opportunity to have sex with him—be it in a park, on a rooftop, or in an abandoned building—they would do it just to be able to say that they did it with him before. Women were always buying him things and throwing themselves at him. I too was drawn to him, and when opportunity presented itself, I made my move.

I had four children when I met JD and his family. His family loved Matt because he was their complexion, but they hated my other children. They would call them "Blackie" or "Tar Baby" or some other name referring to Blackness. Sometimes, JD's mother would tease one of her own daughters by saying that she has "nigger hair". Her daughter would get visibly upset, and her mother and the rest of her family members would laugh. Then, her mother would comfort her by saying, "Ah, come on! Look at them!" She would point to my kids and say, "You have good hair compared to *that*!"

Most of the time when we visited his family, they would all speak Spanish so I couldn't understand what they were saying about me and the kids. I allowed JD's sixteen-year-old sister to baby-sit the kids a few times until one night when I went to pick up the kids and saw that Craig Jr. had been beaten in the face. How could they do this to a one-year-old? I was so upset that I started cussin' everybody in the house. I could have tolerated them beating my other kids, but not Craig Jr. Somebody was gonna pay for this! JD's mother called the police on me, and when they arrived, she spoke to them in Spanish. According to the officer, she'd said that I mistreat my children and should have them taken away from me. The cops saw Craig Jr.'s battered, little face and questioned the other kids. According to the other kids, everyone was given food except Lil Craig. For him, a piece of chicken was put on the table, and every time he picked it up, either the baby-sitter or her mother would beat him. He was hungry, and they never told him not to take it. No one was arrested, but from that day on, I never left my children with JD's family. I also promised Lil Craig that I would *never* leave him

again.

One day in 1977, JD's mother wanted the two of us to visit her. I left the kids with my sister, and JD and I went to his mother's house. When we got there, there was a girl and a guy in the living room. I had never seen them before, so I didn't know who they were. The girl was ready to fight JD because she wanted to know who *I* was. It turned out that the girl was an ex-girlfriend of JD's. She and JD had a child together, but she was involved and living with some other guy. JD's mother wanted to get him and the girl back together. The guy in the room was also an "ex-girlfriend" of JD's. Apparently, JD was with *him* before he had ever met the girl. While the girl and guy were yelling and arguing about *me*, JD got a phone call from yet another ex-girlfriend. This one had stopped seeing him when she found out that he was sleeping with guys. Everyone suddenly wanted to be back in his life because his mother had called and told them that a dead relative left him a lot of money. She obviously wanted him to be with *anyone* but me.

JD was no longer the man I'd thought he was. I

had had enough. I walked out and started looking for another place to live. I didn't know it at the time, but I was pregnant with my fifth child. Once I'd found out, it didn't take long for word to get back to JD. He started coming to my new home and stealing from me. He even tried to move into my home with a young girl one time. By this time, word was out that he was sleeping with a lot of girls and guys right in our neighborhood. The women knew that he was sleeping with girls, boys, men, and other women, but they still flocked to him. I couldn't understand it because it wasn't hard for me to decide to leave him alone. All I'd ever seen in him was gone in a single moment. Once again, I moved to a new place.

Toward the end of 1977, my son Durell was born. Somehow, JD found out where I was living and broke into my home with another guy after I came home with the baby. He smacked me around, and the other guy pulled a knife on me. They both stole a bunch of my things to sell, and—before leaving—JD told me that I had better not call the police. He said that if I *did,* he would come back and shoot some dope into my baby's vein and kill him. It was one thing for *my* life to be threatened, but now my children were in danger.

I contacted the Bureau of Child Welfare and explained my situation. I wanted them to keep my children until I could get away from JD and find a new place to live. BCW sent a couple of representatives to interview me and the children, and then a date was set for them to take the kids into their custody. By then, I had had second thoughts and finally changed my mind. I'd decided to keep the kids and just move out of the area. I don't know *who* was doing it, but someone kept calling BCW and telling them they needed to take my children *anyway.* Before this could happen, my oldest daughter disappeared. I went into a deep depression because I didn't know if JD had found out what I was planning and decided to get to the children *first*—starting with Janice. We looked for her for weeks, and then one day the police called me to view the body of an eight-year-old girl that was found dead in Prospect Park. We lived right in front of Prospect Park at the time, so I was afraid that the murdered little girl was my Janice—but it wasn't. That little corpse would be soaked with some other mother's tears.

The police informed me that they were giving up their search because they believed my sisters knew where Janice was but weren't cooperating. Maybe that was why I'd been rushed out of their homes whenever I visited them. I went to my sisters, and they finally admitted that Janice *was* with them but was recently sent to a small town in Florida to live with my mother and grandmother. This town was called High Springs. They said they sent her there because they didn't want her to be sent to the children's shelter. I was *so* upset with them. It would have been better if they'd just told me. My daughter's disappearance had me so stressed that I'd become physically ill, so I agreed to allow BCW to take the rest of my children. I really needed to gather my strength, so this was the best thing to do at the time.

Now, I was alone. After constantly moving and

then being robbed by JD, I didn't have the means to move right away. I removed all of the lightbulbs in the hallway so no one could see me come or go. I nailed down my windows and—because I dared not use the lights in the apartment—hung dark blankets over them so that the candlelight I quietly lived by wouldn't give me away. I kept my door locked and never responded when anyone knocked on it. I worked the late shift at my job so the block would be empty whenever I got home. I figured that if I kept this up for a few weeks, JD would think I moved and would finally stop coming around. Only then would I be free to walk in the light of day again.

I avoided daylight like a vampire for a whole month before JD finally believed that I was gone. At that time, I had enough money to get another place, which was near my job. I then contacted BCW about getting my children back but found that it wouldn't happen immediately. I would have to visit my children twice a month for six months, during which time BCW wanted to make sure that JD was gone for good. Unfortunately, JD somehow found out where

I worked and followed me home one night. Once again, I couldn't get rid of him, so I had no choice but to let him stay. In a month, I had nothing, and every pay day my check was spent before I'd ever received it. I couldn't pay rent or buy groceries, so we had to move into a single room occupancy. Once ownership changed hands, people were getting paid to leave our new home, but I never received a check. The building was almost empty when JD started staying away from home. It started with two to four days, but then he started staying away for two or three weeks. I never knew how long he would be gone, but I had enough sense to know that this was the break that I needed.

The next time JD came home and left, I made a run for it. I left everything I had as well as a note saying that I was moving to North Carolina. A month later, I tiptoed back into the building to get some of my things. To my surprise, JD hadn't been there at all. I rewrote the note so it would look like I'd *just* left it. A week later, I showed up to get the last of my belongings. It was a chance I should not have taken. Someone told JD that I'd left but would come back to get some things from time to time. When I entered the room this time, the bastard was waiting for me and wouldn't let me leave. I stayed away from work for three days because he made me go everywhere that he went to keep me from leaving him. On that third night, he left the room. I watched him walk down the block from the window. As soon as he turned the corner, I was out of the building and running in the opposite direction. I got the *hell* out of that neighborhood. This time, I'd have to do without anything that I'd left behind because there was no way that I was going back.

I didn't see JD for quite a while—that is, until he showed up at my job. He and four other guys trapped my boss and I in a top floor office as we were locking up one night. They started breaking things with their baseball bats, and JD threatened to hurt my sick, old boss if I didn't leave with him and his boys. My boss was brave and defiant. He declared that I didn't have to go *anywhere* with them. This resulted in them swinging their bats at my boss like a bunch of crazy fools, but that didn't stop him from trying to protect me. He knew that I'd been trying to get away from JD for months. Unfortunately, the odds were against us. I could see that JD and his crew were high on dope and would stop at nothing, so I agreed to go with them on the condition that they wait downstairs and outside the building so that my boss and I could finish locking up for the night. They agreed because they knew that there was only one way in or out of the building. Once they'd made their noisy exit, my boss and I called the police. We stalled for an hour, but the police never arrived. The guys started getting rowdy again, so I had no choice but to leave with them. They took me to an old, abandoned building on Parkside. It was near Prospect Park and behind a McDonald's. I wasn't allowed outside because people in the neighborhood might recognize me. I wasn't allowed near windows, either.

I could tell that JD didn't trust the other guys, but I could also tell that they were afraid of him. He would leave me with them and *dare* them to touch me; they never did. One of the guys looked like a building with legs and arms, and the scar on his left temple matched the scowl that was always on his face. Another of my abductors was short and portly and always looked as if he had seen a ghost. The other two weren't as tall as JD, but they came very close. One of them—the one that looked like the youngest of the group—had a little more mass than him, and the other was skinny. Although a couple of the guys looked as if they could go the distance with JD and possibly win, they never challenged him.

For seven days, I was forced to stay on a small mattress in a closet. The only time I was let out was when I had to go to the bathroom, and even *then* the door was guarded. Naturally, I tried to escape through the bathroom window, but I had a little too much booty for that...thanks mom!I often found myself spending a lot of time trying to find another way out of the bathroom, but whenever I was in there too long, the guys would start beating on the door and yelling for me to get out of there—so much for my great escape!

Through small cracks in the closet door, I could

see that JD blocked the room door with an old refrigerator once everyone was inside. The youngest guy in the group was the only one allowed to come and go—other than JD—because he had a job and made sure that the guys had food to eat. He had to enter and exit by way of fire escape, but King JD would simply order his lowly servants to remove the refrigerator whenever *he* wished to exit or enter.

The youngest guy was nice to me. He would open the closet door and sit and talk to me. That's how I found out his name was Paco. The other guys were too afraid to say a word to me, but Paco wasn't. He even asked them to let me go, but they were too afraid of getting beat up by JD. Since that didn't work, Paco convinced them to let me sit in the room for a change because it was hot in the closet. The other guys agreed but kept their distance. Then, on the fifth day, Paco somehow managed to convince them to allow him to take me outside so I could get a little fresh air. He had them remove the refrigerator from the door so the trip outside would be easier for me. Once outside, he allowed me to make a call from a payphone on the corner. I called my boss, who was worried sick about me. I asked him if the police had been there. He said they never came—not even after he reported that I had been taken from the job against my will. He said that when he went to the precinct to complain, he was told that neither a call nor a report of a missing person had been received. It was obvious that they were not going to help, so I told my boss where I was and that I would try to escape that night. I told him that I wouldn't go back to the jobsite because JD would just come and get me again. My boss assured me that my job would always be there if I wanted or needed it, and he told me to be careful. At that point, the receiver was snatched from my hand and slammed down. It was JD. I told him I tried to call my sister to get some money but she wasn't home. JD grabbed me by my arm and then started yelling at Paco in Spanish, and—to my surprise—Paco yelled back. They had a heated argument that ended in Paco being sent away. JD then forced me back into the building. He made me take off my clothes and shoes and get back into the closet. He then told the other guys that he had somewhere to go and that they'd better not let me out of the closet again. A couple of hours later, he returned with a boy who must have been about thirteen or fourteen years old. The boy was bruised and looked scared. JD told the guys to go to a room on the next floor of the building and to stay there for an hour and a half. After the guys left the room, JD punched and slapped the boy, who insisted that he'd given him all the money he had. I guess the boy's bleeding and sobbing were a turn-on for JD. What he did next I can't bring myself to discuss. I backed away from the crack in the closet door and cried myself to sleep as the boy's muffled screams called no one to his rescue.

I awoke to the sound of movement in the room. When I peered through the crack, there was no sign of the boy, but JD was now dragging two girls by the arm and toward the closet. The door opened, and they were thrust into my world. Shortly after, two men walked into the room, and JD's crew was sent away for the rest of the night. While the Sodomite fed his carnal appetite, I quietly tried to open the closet door...but it felt like it was locked. Escape seemed futile, so I began talking to my new roommates in hopes of forming an alliance and escaping through our united efforts. At first, they didn't want to talk, but when they realized I was bent on escaping they opened up to me. I found that they were sisters. Tasha was fourteen, and Tina was fifteen. They said that JD had done this to them before but individually. They said sometimes he would make them get money from family members or friends to give to him. Other times, they had to endure beatings and rapes. They were so afraid of him but felt that the three of us would be strong enough to get out of there together. Together we planned to pretend to have to go to the bathroom one by one once JD and the two catamites were tired and resting. With the other guys gone and JD worn out, there *had* to be a window of opportunity. We began tapping the door and calling out. JD got up, opened the closet door, and told Tina to hurry up so the next girl could go. He said that after the second one returned, then the third should go and then we should all shut up for the rest of the night or he would shut us up. After giving us these instructions, he lay back down with his boyfriends and fell into a deep sleep. From the hallway, Tina peeked into the room and motioned for Tasha to make her exit. After quickly glancing at the guys and hearing JD's thunderous snores, Tasha hurried to her sister's side. Then, they motioned for me. I stepped out of the closet looking for my clothing and shoes. Upon scanning the room, my eyes quickly locked onto a pair of eyes that were staring back at me; it was one of the boyfriends. I thought for sure that he was going to wake JD and tell him that we were trying to leave because I saw that he was holding my clothes in one hand and my shoes in the other. Fear rendered my body motionless. Slowly, the guy got up and walked toward me. He handed me my clothing, and I quickly dressed myself. When he handed me my shoes, I saw that he'd placed some money in them. I put the money in my pocket and quietly thanked him as I put the shoes upon my feet. The two of us tiptoed to the door. He whispered that we should hurry up and leave and that he'd be on the lookout should JD awake. Once outside the building, we girls ran like cheetahs. They went their way, and I went mine. I would never see them again, and I know we all hoped never to see JD again.

I was so relieved when I finally made it home. I found comfort in knowing that JD still didn't know where I lived. Finally, I could bathe and fix a good meal. It felt good to indulge in the little things once again. I didn't go back to work for a while. My boss told me that JD would be outside the building day and night watching and waiting for me. After about a month, he'd finally given up. I didn't trust it, though, so I continued to stay away.

About a year after my escape, my son Matt was to return to me from the Children's Village. I had a little money in the bank, so I moved to a very nice, quiet place where Matt could have his own bedroom. Although JD didn't know where I was staying, I lived in constant fear. I was afraid he would find me... afraid of the havoc he would wreak upon my children and I once they were returned to me. I had to keep a low profile until I could be certain that the nightmare was indeed over. My sister Wilmer stayed in touch [as always], and when Brandee moved in with her, Wilmer could finally afford a telephone of her own. This allowed us to talk more often than in the past, and being able to express my feelings with her and Brandee made me feel like a human again.

One night, Wilmer came over and asked me to go to this church with her. She said she'd been going there for a while and that I would love it. I asked where the church was and found that it was in that same neighborhood that JD was in. I wasn't going to go, but she convinced me that I didn't have to worry about him because he'd left the area a long time ago. I still was hesitant, but she spoke with such conviction. "Why would you let that monster come between you and your God?" she asked. "Don't you know that God knows about all the shit JD did? That's probably why no one has seen or heard from him in so long. His ass is probably burning in Hell as we speak…stinking up the place! Got Hell smelling like hot ass!" We laughed, and once I was dressed, we were on our way. Needless to say, as soon as we exited the subway on the street level, JD was right there waiting for us. He grabbed me and started dragging me away. I was kicking and screaming, but no one helped me. I yelled for Wilmer to follow us and then call the police, but she just stood there until I could no longer see her anymore. JD dragged me into a building that he was living in, forced me into his apartment, and threw me onto the floor before locking the door. He knelt over me with each knee pinning one of my arms to the floor. I was unable to defend myself as he beat me repeatedly while threatening to cut me up and throw the pieces from the roof. He said no one would ever know that he killed me because the stray dogs out there would wolf down the chunks before anyone could suspect anything. He also said that if anyone *did* question him about my death, he would say I committed suicide because he chose a *guy* over me.

The door opened with a creak. His lover was home, and after seeing me battered, bruised, and bloody with a JD medallion on my chest, he wanted to know what the hell JD was doing. JD jumped up, pushed him aside, locked the door, and ordered me to take off my clothes. I couldn't move. I tried, but my arms were dead; my body hurt; and my eyes were practically swollen shut. My lack of response cost me two more punches to my face. His lover became outraged when JD started tearing my clothes from my body. He pushed JD off me, and then the two of them started yelling and fighting. I couldn't see much, but I heard things breaking around me. I heard the hits, and I heard a body hit the floor. Then his lover was crying about having lived with him for a year. "I bought you whatever you needed!" he sobbed. "I took you wherever you wanted to go! *I* gave you money! *I* bought your dope, and *this* is how you treat me???" I heard another hit...then everything was silent. I soon felt JD's hot, stinking breath on my face, and I thanked God that my body was numb. I was spared the anguish of feeling him inside me. He tried to push through me...tried to make me cry out, but my body was just a shell. It seemed like I wasn't even in it because I didn't feel a thing. When he was done with me, I heard him plop down on the bed. I prayed for Death to carry me away from it all, but even *he* wouldn't hear my cry. When I prayed for God to have mercy on me, I heard a shuffling in the room. I heard what sounded like a thick frying pan hit something three times. JD's lover helped me to my feet, into a robe, and out of the building. He said we were going to the police and that JD was gonna pay. The police called an ambulance, and I was rushed to the hospital while JD's lover told them what he'd witnessed. The next day, the police came to speak with me, and I told them all that had happened. I recited Wilmer's phone number and said she could confirm what I said about being abducted. One of the cops went to make the call. He returned with a grim, puzzled look on his face and said he'd spoken with Wilmer. As the cop recited her version of events, I was flabbergasted. She told him that JD was there when we left the train station and that he pleaded for me to take him back. She said he and I walked away all hugged up and that there was kissing and speaking…not kicking and screaming. She claimed not to know anything about any abduction and that she thought JD and I were going to his place for make up sex. When I heard those words, I realized that it was her all along. *She* was the reason JD kept finding me in the past. *She* was the reason that I was in the hospital. I don't know why, but she had set me up. Instead of taking me to church, she escorted me straight to Hell.

After my treatment in the hospital, the police wanted me to return to the place where JD confined me and wait for them to arrive. I told them I didn't want to because if JD were to see me, I think he would just shoot me. Going back there would be too dangerous. They told me I *had* to do it. I told them I was *not* going back there unless they went *with* me. There was no way I was going to wait for them like a duck in hunting season. After all, they never showed up when called before. The police insisted I go there and said they'd meet me. I was tired of arguing about this, so I said ok just to shut them up. I then went home to take a nice, long, relaxing bath. If anything, *I* would meet *them* there. As I got dressed after bathing, I saw a commercial advertising Victim Services. I wrote down the phone number, dialed it, and told them my situation. They were very helpful. Before I could hang up the phone, six of their police cars had arrived outside my home. One of the officers told me they were there to return to the scene with me. I told them the crossroads, and we were on our way. When we got to the location, we all went inside. Unfortunately, JD wasn't there. A long wait proved to be fruitless, so after hours and hours I decided to go home. A couple of the officers escorted me back to my place and said that in the afternoon they wanted me to work with a sketch artist so they could come up with a physical profile of Jorge Delvera. They said they were going to comb the streets until he was found and then bring him to justice. I got some rest, and the officers got their profile. I felt good about leaving the matter in their hands. They truly wanted to get this man off the streets. Now that they knew what he looked like, I could continue living life. The officers said they would call me for a positive ID once JD was located...

Two years after making that call to Victim Services, I was waiting on a corner for a stoplight to change so I could cross the street. That's when I saw JD walking toward me. He looked like the dope had dried him up. He was skinny before, but now he was just skeletal. As he got closer to me, I panicked within. My heart went into overdrive; my limbs stiffened; and scenes from my life with this monster dashed through my mind. This Demon of Carnality should have been in jail or dead somewhere with a needle jammed in his arm! But there he was walking the streets…bones rattling and eyes looking like they wanted to leap from their sockets with every step he took! I thought, "If he says *one* word to me, we're just gonna have to go at it right here and right now 'cause I can't take it no more! I'm tired of running and hiding! I'm tired of being hit! Most of all, I'm tired of not knowing *when* he would pop up and *what* he would do! It's gonna take all the strength I have to fight this fight, so God be with me! Lord, just help me to make a fist and maybe knock one of them eyes loose!" JD was now at arm's length. It was now or never! Our eyes met like those of duelers of the Wild West before drawing their pistols. He looked me right in the face…and kept walking. He didn't even recognize me! What a blessed day! This man put me through years of pure hell…*hell*, I tell ya! I don't know if he was ever arrested for the things he did to me or to others, and I no longer cared. I just knew that I didn't have to worry about him anymore. I could finally come and go as I pleased. I could get my children back. My life would begin anew. To this day, JD still haunts my dreams, but even there he has no power. He's just a vision of an unpleasant past… unable to hurt me in any way…strengthening me by the fact that I survived. Yes, it *was* Hell, but I thank God for making me invisible in the eye of the demon.

CHAPTER SEVEN

The Lying King

There have been a couple more guys in my life since the ones mentioned here, and whenever I got tired of getting beat on by one of them, I just moved to the next guy. Their fists spoke a language I heeded but didn't understand. I really wanted to understand why no one would love me. I wanted to understand why a man would go to another woman even though I treated him like a king. I wanted to understand why a man would want to hit me rather than hold me. What was it under my surface that made a man want to beat off my blackness? I may never know, but I've learned that the fist is never satisfied; neither is the heart.

Walter didn't start out the way that he is now. He was my Knight in Shining Armor. One night back in 1987, I had gone down to the club because I found out that my boyfriend-at-the-time was there with another woman. He was upset and embarrassed that I'd confronted him in front of all those people, so he started beating on me right then and there. Walter came to my rescue, and we've been an item ever since. Every night, I would go to the club and Walter would be there making sure that my ex didn't lay a finger on me. We danced. We talked. We laughed. We drank like the fish in the sea. He never hid the fact that he had a wife and kids at home, and he *couldn't* hide the fact that he was messing with Big Butt Aretha on the side. What I liked about him was that those things didn't matter; what mattered was me. It was like I had become the most important person in his life.

By the beginning of 1988, Walter and his wife had separated, and other guys started juggling Aretha's butt once Walter moved in with me. Walter had chosen *me* over his wife and over his constant flame, and that made me feel special.

Year after year, we drank and danced the night away after a long day of work, but in 1991 things began to change. Walter would leave for work in the morning and not come home until midnight. Once home, he would say that the car broke down. His car would break down three times per week after that. I wanted to know what was going on, but he would insist that there was nothing to tell. "Nuthin's goin' on," he'd say. "What, ya think I'm cheatin' on you? I don't know how you could even *think* that I would cheat on you. My car is a piece of crap, that's all. I wasn't keepin' count of how many times a week it broke down, but as soon as I could *afford* to, I'll get another one. You know I wanna get home as fast as I can after work so I could squeeze your meat!" At that point, he would squeeze my butt, tickle me, and then chase me around the bedroom. All of my doubts would fade, and he would be mine…for a couple of nights.

Walter worked every day but never had any money. My salary had to cover all of the bills and our daily expenses. It seemed like he tried to make up for this by being helpful: he would offer to go to the store for me to get something I needed to finish cooking dinner, and I wouldn't see him again until four the next morning.

Our sex life was suffering most of all...at least mine was. Walter and I used to have sex several times *every* night, but at this point he could only manage to do it once if at all. If he *did* manage to do it once, that would be it for the week. When I questioned these changes, the whole relationship took a massive turn. Walter would cuss me out and speak to me as if I were nothing at all. He would hit me and then storm out of the house. After that, every time he wanted to lay up with some other woman, he would start a fight with me and leave. While he was gone, I would think about leaving him, but then I would realize that a lot of the things we fought about were *my* fault. For example, he would claim my children on his tax return, and after a while I would get on his case about him not giving me any of that money. I was yelling at him about not sharing that money with me, and the man had never even received his refund! How wrong was that?!? Another time, the whole town was talking about him hitting the lotto for $5,500, and I got on his case again since he had not been paying his share of the bills. It turns out that *he* wasn't the person that hit the number; it was Walter Blackmon. If I hadn't listened to he said she said, that fight could have been avoided and we would have spent the next four days together instead of apart. I was always wrong, and if the shoe was on the other foot I know *I* would get upset each time a rumor led to friction in my home. He continued to put up with me in spite of my insecurities. He must have had a lot of love for me.

Considering my track record, I started thinking twice about approaching Walter with things I had heard. Instead of going to him, I would just push the rumor to the back of my mind and have a drink. Sometimes the rumors would coincide with Walter's absence from our home. In those cases, I drank twice as much. Before I knew it, the daily pangs of life were causing me to go through a case of beer [that's 24 cans, for you non-drinkers] each day. I was never drunk, though. There wasn't enough alcohol in a case to get *me* drunk. Walter could stay gone all he wanted as long as I had my beer.

Whenever Walter *was* around and I had been

drinking, his behavior was very different. He would come home from work early every day and sweet – talk me into believing I was so important to him. I thought for sure that I was finally seeing the real side of him. As long as I drank, he would come home and he would be nice to me, and *that* was what I wanted. Beer gave me back my man, so I had no desire to leave it alone. I had developed such confidence in Walter that the rumors about all those other women didn't matter to me anymore. What mattered was that he was with *me* and not *them*. If I were getting low on beer, he would run out and return in record time with a couple more cases. We talked. We laughed. He was in love with me, and I was *so* in love with him. In spite of all the things people were saying about him, I would be at ease whenever he walked into the house. I went through a lot of changes with my children, but that's another story. Through it all, Walter was by my side—beer in hand—and I just knew that he cared for me more than any of my children ever could.

By 1997, my youngest daughter had spoken to me about some of the things I did while drunk... things she didn't like...things that pushed her away from me. I don't remember ever being drunk, nor do I remember doing any of the things she claimed I did. I *never* beat her with an extension cord! I *never* walked into the living room while she was watching tv, smacked her in the face with all my might, and then left the room without saying a word! I *never* called her a klutz, and I *never* told her that she was getting dumber and dumber every day! And how the *hell* could I have *possibly* slipped on a potato peel on a *carpeted* floor?!? The things she said I did just didn't make sense. I *never* abruised my kids. Why would she say things to hurt me? "Ma," she said, "you *did* abuse us. What I told you wasn't even the half of it! Just because you don't remember or you don't believe you could have done these things, it doesn't change the fact that they happened. It was so bad that I told myself that once I graduated from high school I was gonna move away from you and never come back. That's why you haven't seen me in all these years. Every time I tried to talk to you about the drinking, you would get to the point where you'd wanna fight me. There was no way that I was gonna hit you, so I dealt with it by staying away from you. I basically wrote you out of my life."

If nothing else, she made me think. And at first, all I could think was, "I'll drink to that!" Then, reality kicked in. People had always asked me what I did to make my daughters not want anything to do with me. Janice and MeLody left and hardly ever called: no "Happy Birthday"…no "Merry Christmas" or "Happy Mother's Day". My oldest son died in 1993, and my youngest son was always calling the Child Abuse people on me. My other son was always here; he wasn't going nowhere…not to school; not to the store [unless I paid him]; and certainly not out into the world to live on his own. I don't know if that was a blessing or a curse, but I started to realize which one the alcohol was.

I finally reached the point in my life when I knew things had to change. I accepted Christ as my Savior and gave up drinking. I was content with my newly found freedom. Walter wasn't, though. He quickly went back to his old ways. He would lie about where he was, and he would lie about where he was going. I kept letting things slide partly because I didn't want to fight and partly because I felt that not bothering him would make him want and appreciate me. Unfortunately, Walter had started drinking so much that fighting was inevitable. Our relationship had become a big disgrace, and I was growing tired of it. I wanted to leave him so badly that it was driving me crazy. Every night, a headache would keep me from sleeping, and I would tell myself that tomorrow would be the day. Procrastinating caused me to still be with him three years later in spite of the many sleepless nights. At that point in our relationship, two things happened…

First, I went to the club looking for him one night. I hadn't seen him in days and wanted to talk about this so-called relationship. He wasn't there, so I left. Aretha's trailer was a short distance from the club, and I saw Walter come out of it as I left the club. I was upset, so I started yelling at him as he lit a cigarette. The lights came on in the trailer, and the door opened. Aretha stood there in lingerie while Walter talked to me like a dog. He even told her to call the police on me. She did better than that, though. She told me that he was *hers* and that I needed to wake up and smell the coffee. She said he pays her rent and all her bills. She said that when he hit the number a few years ago, he took her to Tampa and they stayed in a nice hotel for four days. She said he also pays her $50 each time he lays with her, and that his tax refund is always her bonus. I was in shock. She was being malicious, so a part of me wanted to see her bleed. I wanted to grab her ankles, yank them towards me, and make her bang the back of her head on the floor or the metal doorway. I realized, though, that—as whorish as she may be— my fight was not with *her*. At first, I stood quietly as I processed her every word and pictured her unconscious in a pool of blood, but then I just stormed away. My eyes were opened. It was truly the end.

I didn't see Walter for a few days after that. He was avoiding me. Finally, he showed up at my house, which brings me to the second biggest event of the year: he proposed to me. At first I didn't know what to feel, but when I realized that he had once again chosen *me,* my answer could only be *yes*! After thirteen years, the world would finally see that he was *mine*! I had won! We had a small but pleasant wedding, after which—I'm sad to say—he picked up where he had left off. The drinking and the beatings continued. I began to enjoy his not being home because it gave my bruises time to heal. Then one night, I found myself being dragged off the sofa by my ankle. This drunken madman dragged me *through* the house, *down* the front steps, and *onto* the lawn where he slurred, "Get out my house, you *bitch*!" before stumbling back inside. I had enough. I made my way back into the house and managed to call the police before Walter could come at me again. Walter was yellin' and cussin' right up until the cop got there. (Our town is so small that it only has *one* policeman.) Then, he had the nerve to put on an innocent act and try to play the victim. In spite of that whole charade, the policeman could see the truth because my bruises were visible and

Walter's breath could start a forest fire on a sunny day. As the Demon of Strife was taken to jail, I began packing my things. Human Resources helped me get an apartment for low rent, and that's where I am right now. Walter wasn't in jail that long, but by the time he was released, I had already moved. My phone number stayed the same, so Walter continues to call. He says he wants us to get back together, but I've had enough. All I have to show for the many years we've been together are bruises and a broken heart. I've wasted almost twenty years of my life with this man, so I can't wait for our divorce to be finalized. So much time has been lost; I can never get it back. I could only pray that I'll make better use of whatever time I have left.

Chapter Eight

Quiet Reflections: This Book of Life and Love

Ever since I left Walter, my health has improved. I didn't know that mental strain could take such a toll on the body! My blood pressure is much lower now, and the headaches that plagued me every other day are a lot less frequent. My body still aches, but that comes with age. The best part is that at night, when I lay my head to pillow, I enter a restful slumber. It feels good to be able to dream again.

Writing has been very good for me. It truly allowed me to vent, which is great because there's no one for me to talk to when I hurt. If I talk to family, they distort my words and gossip about me. Experience has taught me that friendship could be merely an illusion, so talking to a friend was out of the question as well. Writing was best because I'm a very private person; I really don't like putting my business out in the street. Once my anger was on paper, I would feel a sense of relief. Yeah, writing was the way to go. If everything were taken away from me, what I felt would still be there. This meant my writing would live on.

I have to admit that I have *major* trust issues. I've always had them, but now I feel they've been justified. I know that some people are trustworthy and others are not, but it's hard to distinguish one from the other since I can't even trust my own judgment. Those that I trusted the most turned out to be the least trustworthy. Those that I'd never dreamed of trusting could have been trusted with all matters of the heart and mind if only I had extended my heart and mind to them. When I openly gave my trust, it was toyed with and then discarded. How could I not withhold my trust after that? I had to be more careful, and the only way I could do that was by not trusting at all. Now, it's a habit that I just can't seem to break. In my mind, trusting just isn't an option. Love really isn't where it's at, either. I loved inspite of the consequences. I loved in spite of the pain. In times that I felt like a winner, I was the biggest loser of all. Maybe it wasn't love. Maybe I called it that for lack of a better word. Regardless, in this book of life and love I didn't give a detailed description of the men for fear of blinding the reader; I didn't want the reader to see the JD in this book but miss the JD in her life. A lot of times, it's easier to see other people's pain and faults while being oblivious to our own. I'm not the only one out there that's hurting, and the men in my life—the men in this book—are reflections of the Legion that swarm the Earth. Other women are being mistreated and either stay or run… but not far enough. A lot of times, those of us who run find ourselves in the arms of the same man over and over again. He looks different, and his name is different…but he is the same. The demons in this book are everywhere. Because of them, I've been unhappy. My failure to recognize them caused me to lose a big part of life and an even bigger part of myself. I realize now that instead of trying to change each situation, I should have been working on changing myself. If I had changed my behavior and my way of thinking, I could have spared myself a lot of pain. I never considered the possibility that maybe I needed to re-evaluate the things I found attractive in a man. I never should have allowed their actions to dictate my emotions, and I should have sought Higher Counsel sooner to restore my inner peace. I don't have all the answers, but at least now I have some understanding of the consequences that befall the self-willed. As I continue this journey of change and restoration, I'm constantly gaining strength as I find myself. It seems my life is just beginning, so I pray that I'll live long enough to enjoy the happiness that now warms my soul. These everyday demons have truly made my life hell on Earth, but the joy I've found is boundless and no one can take it away from me. What once had dominion over me now lies at my feet. It can't stand before the person I've become, so it seeks the person I used to be. This person's appearance and name are different, but she and I are the same. Keep watch because you just might be the apple of a demon's eye.

THE END

FOREVER FREE

The kiss of Death upon my lips,

my life flows through my fingertips.

My soul soaring the endless sky,

to all Alive, I say good-bye.

The Breath of Life has gone away.

I breathe no more this very day.

My mind...confused.

My heart...a wreck...

love's shadowy, cold silhouette.

To love someone wholeheartedly

is suicide of first degree.

To grasp love within open arms

is sure to cause some lifelong harm.

The pain, I've wreaked upon myself

for always loving someone else.

The death of me...caused by a man

and in it. I lent my own hand.

My heart, my soul, my love I gave

and when I loved, dug my own grave.

The cold dirt now doth cover me,

but I am set forever free.

Family or gender violence does not have to be the norm in your household. There is help for those who would like to restore the peace at home. For support, please contact:

CONNECT

P. O. Box 20217

Greeley Square Station

New York, NY 10001-0006

Main #: (212) 683-0015

Fax #: (212) 683-0016

E-mail: connect@connectnyc.org

Online: connectnyc.org

You could be the one to break the cycle.

ACKNOWLEDGMENTS

Life has been and continues to be an uphill journey. At times, I feel I just don't have the strength to plan my next course or take that next step. It is during these times that I am most thankful for having been fed the Word of God early in life because it allows me to draw strength enough to keep pressing on. Thank you, Maranatha Tabernacle, for preaching the undiluted Word of God.

As a foster child who has grown to adulthood, I realize that God's favor has been upon my life since the beginning, and for that I thank Him. He took me out of the hands of misery and placed me with the Kenny family, and because of that I am here today with hopes of tomorrow. My heartfelt thanks to: Mae, who soars with the angels; Melvin E. Kenny Sr., my father of gold; Leslie P. Kenney, my sister and friend;Melvin E. Kenny II, my wonderful brother; the knowledgeable Karyl, my sister-in-law; my cousin Sheri and her husband Kevin Harrington, whose combined efforts make music that touches the soul.My cousin, Pastor James C. Blocker and his wife Wandra Blocker, teachers of the Word; my cousins Tashanta, James, Tanya, Robert, Tamara, Tracy and Kim; my nieces Daneasha, Marquia, Amanda, and Christian; my nephews, Melvin E. Kenny III and Michael McKinnly Smith, Jr.; and the entire Kenny and Blocker families.

I also extend my gratitude to my brother, Mickey. Your pride in me has always been my joy. May you rest in peace.

I simply *must* thank the Verizon JFK Enterprise group. You'll are like family. I thank you for believing in me and my abilities. I especially want to thank Ms. Wanda for the referral to Kathy Harley, who put me on to blakgirl publishing.com, Inc. Thank you, Kathy, and blakgirl publishing for making this book a reality. And to Rex, all I can say is, "Long Time!"

Last—but certainly not least—I'd like to thank my mother. Thank you for your trials and for your triumphs.

ABOUT THE AUTHOR

MeLinda Smith currently resides in Jamaica, New York. While MeLinda has completed many accomplishments in her life, she has now added becoming a writer to her profile. Although "Everyday Demons" is her first novel, she has certainly proved herself to be a "brilliant", sought after writer on the literary scene.